Advanced Training for Scrum Masters and Agile Coaches

Part of the Agile Education Series™

Notes:

Copyright Notice 2015.

‣ Unless otherwise noted, these materials and the presentation of them are based on the methodology developed by Cape Project Management, Inc. and are copyrighted materials of Cape Project Management, Inc., which are used with its permission. Cape Project Management, Inc. reserves all its rights.

‣ "PMI", "PMP" and "PMI-ACP" are service, certification and trademarks registered in the United States and other nations.

‣ "PSM I" is a trademark of Scrum.org

‣ All other brand or product names used in this presentation are the trade names or registered trademarks of their respective owners.

2   Copyrighted material. 2015

Agile Project
Management Training

Notes:

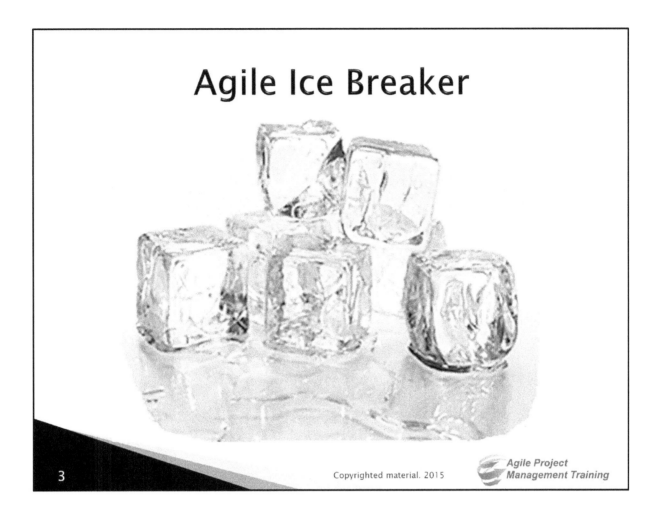

Agile Ice Breaker

Copyrighted material. 2015

Agile Project
Management Training

3

Notes:

Introductions and Expectations Using Affinity Mapping

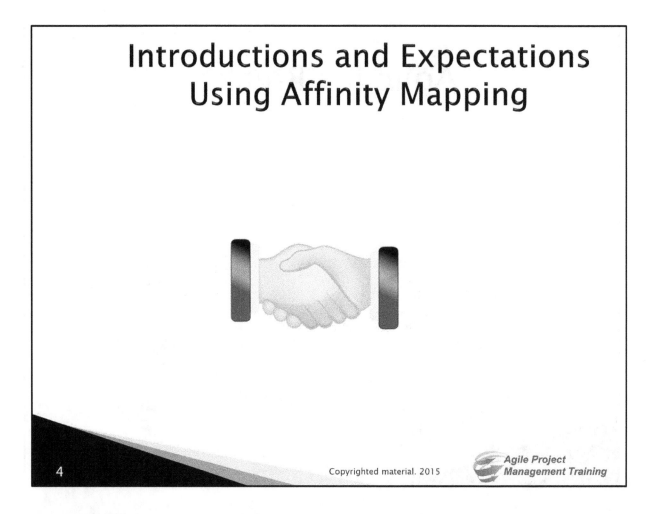

Copyrighted material. 2015

4

Agile Project
Management Training

Notes:

About Us

- The course curriculum developed by Dan Tousignant, CSP of Cape Project Management, Inc.
- Provides public and onsite training:
  - BostonAgileTraining.com
  - AgileProjectManagementTraining.com
- Follow us on Twitter @ScrumDan
- The content of this course is licensed to your instructor

5

Copyrighted material. 2015

Agile Project Management Training

Notes:

Agile Education Series™

‣ Scrum Master Training
‣ Advanced Scrum Master Training
‣ Product Owner and User Story Training
‣ Kanban & Agile
‣ PMI–ACP® Agile Exam Preparation
‣ How to implement Agile in your organization
‣ Agile for Team Members
‣ Agile for Executives

6   Copyrighted material. 2015    Agile Project
                                                                                 Management Training

Notes:

Continuing Education

▸ This course provides education credits for the following educations or certifications:
  ◦ Continuing Certification for PMPs & PMI-ACPs: 7 PDUs Category B: Continuing Education
  ◦ PMI-ACP Application: 7 Agile Education Contact Hours
  ◦ Scrum Alliance SEUs for CSP Application and Maintenance: 7 SEUS Category C: Outside Events

7

Copyrighted material. 2015

 Agile Project Management Training

Notes:

Course Objectives

- Assumes you have already completed typical Scrum Master training.
- Give you an opportunity to assess your organization and yourself
- Learn advanced Agile best practices
- Gain knowledge for the PSM I Exam
- Have fun!

8

Copyrighted material. 2015

Agile Project Management Training

Notes:

Agenda

Day 1
Agility Assessments
The Scrum Master Role
Advance Scrum Techniques
Implementing Agile
PSM I and Class Review

9

Copyrighted material. 2015

Agile Project Management Training

Notes:

Announcements

- ‣ Participant materials
  - ◦ Slides
  - ◦ Exercises
- ‣ Facilities orientation
- ‣ Breaks
- ‣ Emergencies

10

Copyrighted material. 2015

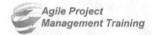 Agile Project
Management Training

Notes:

What is an Agile Maturity Model?

▸ A model that is designed to enhance and improve Agile practices by assessing the current state of your organization

▸ A way to determine how closely you adhere to Agile principles

▸ A model which shows your organization on an Agile maturity continuum from an initial or ad-hoc level to a continuously improving, self-sustaining level

11

Copyrighted material. 2015

 *Agile Project Management Training*

Notes:

Agile Maturity Matrix

Level 1 Ad Hoc Agile	Level 2 Doing Agile	Level 3 Being Agile	Level 4 Thinking Agile	Level 5 Culturally Agile
• Agile is either not used or used inconsistently across organization • Variable quality • Predominantly manual testing • Success achieved through heroic individual efforts	• Teams start to exhibit some consistent Agile habits • Knowledge sharing begins to occur across teams • Agile tools and practices is common • Quality improves	• Most of the project portfolio is Agile • Role and responsibilities are consistent across teams • Disciplined, repeatable processes are in place with high quality results • Respect for people and continuous improvement is occurring	• Agile habits at a high maturity across the organization • Successful use of Agile at Scale • Success across multiple geographies • Measurement systems in place to track business value realization • Test and build automation is highly enabled	• Lean and Agile are part of the organizational culture • Perfecting waste reduction, lack of overburden and inefficiency and a smooth flow of delivery • Sustainable pace of innovation • Continuous organizational learning and optimization of work process
0–80	81–160	161–240	240–320	+++

12

Copyrighted material. 2015

Agile Project Management Training

Notes:

ACTIVITY

Agile Assessment Results

Prior to class, take the Agile Assessment at:
http://bit.ly/AgileAssessment

Copyrighted material. 2015

Agile Project
Management Training

13

Notes:

Sample Agile Assessment

Summary:

You scored 260 out of 320 in the Agile Self-Assessment. Based upon the responses and the following scoring model, Cartera has clearly fulfilled the "Being Agile" criteria and is in the process of maturing into a "Thinking Agile" organization. The three responses in this survey that are the most powerful indicators of Agility are:

You consistently deliver working, tested software every 30 days or less
Each release is driven by business need
Each Sprint you are continuously improving

There are opportunities that exist and should be considered as part of the commitment to be a continuously improving organization.

Level 1 Ad Hoc Agile	Level 2 Doing Agile	Level 3 Being Agile	Level 4 Thinking Agile	Level 5 Culturally Agile
• Agile is either not used or used inconsistently across organization • Variable quality • Predominantly manual testing • Success achieved through heroic individual efforts	• Teams start to exhibit some consistent Agile habits • Knowledge sharing begins to occur across teams • Agile tools and practices is common • Quality improves	• Most of the project portfolio is Agile • Role and responsibilities are consistent across teams • Disciplined, repeatable processes are in place with high quality results • Respect for people and continuous improvement is occurring	• Agile habits at a high maturity across the organization • Successful use of Agile at Scale • Success across multiple geographies • Measurement systems in place to track business value realization • Test and build automation is highly enabled	• Lean and Agile are part of the organizational culture • Perfecting waste reduction, lack of overburden and inefficiency and a smooth flow of delivery • Sustainable pace of innovation • Continuous organizational learning and optimization of work process
0–80	81–160	161–240	240–320	+++

260

DISCUSSION

What can you do to advance your Agile practice?

14

Copyrighted material. 2015

Agile Project
Management Training

Notes:

| |
| |
| |
| |
| |
| |
| |
| |

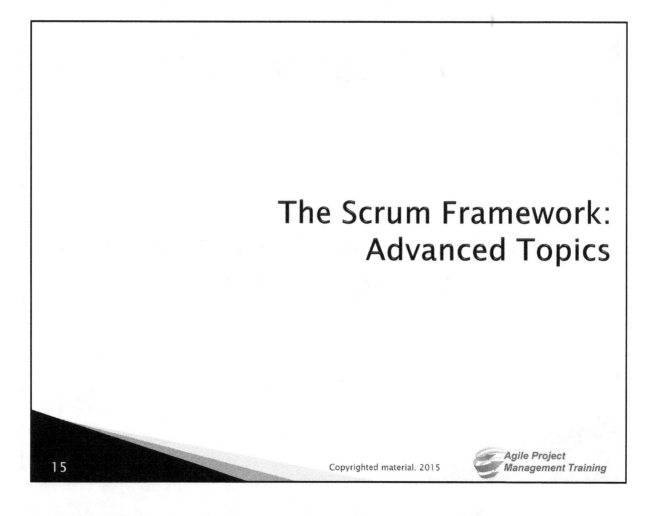

The Scrum Framework:
Advanced Topics

15

Copyrighted material. 2015

Agile Project
Management Training

Notes:

5 Core Values of Scrum

1. **Commitment** – When we, as a team, value the commitment we make to ourselves and our teammates, we are much more likely to give our all to meet our goals.

2. **Focus** – When we value Focus, and devote the whole of our attention to only a few things at once, we deliver a better quality product, faster.

3. **Openness** – When we value being Open with ourselves and our teammates, we feel comfortable inspecting our behavior and practices, we can adapt them accordingly.

4. **Respect** – When we value Respect, people feel safe to voice concerns and discuss issues, knowing that their voices are heard and valued.

5. **Courage** – When we value Courage, people are encouraged to step outside of their comfort zones and take on greater challenges, knowing they will not be punished if they fail.

16

Copyrighted material. 2015

Agile Project Management Training

Notes:

The Role of the Scrum Master

17

Copyrighted material. 2015

Agile Project
Management Training

Notes:

Scrum Master – Top 5

1. Coach team members
2. Manage conflict
3. Facilitate decision making
4. Remove team impediments
5. Increase organizational awareness of Scrum

18

Copyrighted material. 2015

Agile Project
Management Training

Notes:

Servant Leadership

- ▸ Critical to building self–organizing teams
- ▸ More difficult, but more rewarding
- ▸ Facilitates the team to address the tasks
- ▸ Fosters an environment that is trusting and respectful
- ▸ Lets the team members propose the approach to make the project a success
- ▸ Provides support, removes obstacles and stays out of the way

19

Copyrighted material. 2015

 *Agile Project Management Training*

Notes:

| |
| |
| |
| |
| |
| |
| |
| |

Leadership in Agile Projects

- ‣ Learn the team members' needs
- ‣ Know the project's requirements.
- ‣ Act for the simultaneous welfare of the team and the project
- ‣ Create an environment of accountability
- ‣ Serve as the central figure in successful project team development
- ‣ Recognize team conflict as a natural step (Forming, Storming, Norming, Performing)

20

Copyrighted material. 2012

 Agile Project Management Training

Notes:

An Agile Leadership Model

Components	Levels
▸ Process Knowledge	▸ Beginner
▸ Technical Skillset	▸ Practitioner
▸ Business Experience	▸ Master
▸ Facilitation Skills	▸ Coach
▸ Training Skills	▸ Expert
▸ Coaching Skills	

21

Copyrighted material. 2015

Agile Project Management Training

Notes:

	Beginner	Practitioner	Master	Coach	Expert
Process Knowledge	Aware of principles and practices. Participated in an Agile project	Understand the principles and practices. Actively working in and improving an Agile project	Can setup and lead an Agile project. Experience as an Iteration Manager/ Scrum Master	Significant Agile project experience in varied environments. Can adapt to suit project environments	Well recognized with the industry and maintain public presence.
Technical Skillset	Work in a team using core skills (BA, Dev, Tester, PM)	Lead of a discipline within a team. Established standard of practice and quality within a team	Remains current with best-practice and industry trends in relevant discipline.	Recognized by peers as a technical expert in relevant discipline.	Creating and publishing new techniques.
Business Experience	Clear understanding of the business, the operating environment and the market	Comfortable discussing business process. Understand factors influencing business success.	Understand market trends and strategy Sought after for business advice and analysis of impacts.	Understand risk, finance and strategic elements that impact business. Experience running a business unit.	Have run a successful business in your industry. Sought after to advise on running business.
Facilitation Skills	Comfortable working with and leading a group. Ad-hoc facilitation of Agile team ceremonies.	Experienced in facilitating group discussion of complex issues. Leads the facilitation of Agile team ceremonies.	Leads multi-day workshops and planning events for large or newly formed teams.	Facilitates sessions involving complex people issues. Facilitates sessions involving multiple stakeholders and conflicting priorities.	Facilitates senior executive sessions and/or large groups of people.
Training Skills	Enjoy helping other learn. Supports learning initiatives within the team environment.	Have some experience delivering training to small teams.	Comfortable delivering training to larger groups. Participate in developing and updating training content.	Significant training experience across multiple courses. Comfortable writing and piloting new course content.	Recognized and sought after as a trainer. Have trained a number of other trainers.
Coaching Skills	Understand the role and difference between coach, mentor and advisor.	Can provide ad-hoc coaching within current team.	Recognized as a leader and am able to follow a simple coaching model for helping people to resolve their own problems.	Adapt coaching style to suit situation, team and staff level. Comfortable coaching peers and executive staff.	Recognized and sought after as a coach not only in Agile but in other areas of work. Capable of coaching C-level executives

22

Notes:

ACTIVITY

Scrum Master
Self-Assessment

23

Copyrighted material. 2015

Agile Project
Management Training

Notes:

Advanced Training for Scrum Masters and Agile Coaches

	Beginner	Practitioner	Master	Coach	Expert
Process Knowledge	Aware of principles and practices. Participated in an Agile project	Understand the principles and practices. Actively working in and improving an Agile project	Can setup and lead an Agile project. Experience as an Iteration Manager/ Scrum Master	Significant Agile project experience in varied environments. Can adapt to suit project environments	Well recognized with the industry and maintain public presence.
Technical Skillset	Work in a team using core skills (BA, Dev, Tester, PM)	Lead of a discipline within a team. Established standard of practice and quality within a team	Remains current with best-practice and industry trends in relevant discipline.	Recognized by peers as a technical expert in relevant discipline.	Creating and publishing new techniques.
Business Experience	Clear understanding of the business, the operating environment and the market	Comfortable discussing business process. Understand factors influencing business success.	Understand market trends and strategy. Sought after for business advice and analysis of impacts.	Understand risk, finance and strategic elements that impact business. Experience running a business unit.	Have run a successful business in your industry. Sought after to advise on running business.
Facilitation Skills	Comfortable working with and leading a group. Ad-hoc facilitation of Agile team ceremonies.	Experienced in facilitating group discussion of complex issues. Leads the facilitation of Agile team ceremonies.	Leads multi-day workshops and planning events for large or newly formed teams.	Facilitates sessions involving complex people issues. Facilitates sessions involving multiple stakeholders and conflicting priorities.	Facilitates senior executive sessions and/or large groups of people.
Training Skills	Enjoy helping other learn. Supports learning initiatives within the team environment.	Have some experience delivering training to small teams.	Comfortable delivering training to larger groups. Participate in developing and updating training content.	Significant training experience across multiple courses. Comfortable writing and piloting new course content.	Recognized and sought after as a trainer. Have trained a number of other trainers.
Coaching Skills	Understand the role and difference between coach, mentor and advisor.	Can provide ad-hoc coaching within current team.	Recognized as a leader and am able to follow a simple coaching model for helping people to resolve their own problems.	Adapt coaching style to suit situation, team and staff level. Comfortable coaching peers and executive staff.	Recognized and sought after as a coach not only in Agile but in other areas of work. Capable of coaching C-level executives

Activity: Agile Self-Assessment

Directions:

1. Review and identify your level for each component of the matrix.
2. What is your highest competency?
3. What competency do you need to work on most?
4. What competency are you strong at but don't really enjoy?
5. Pair-up and review

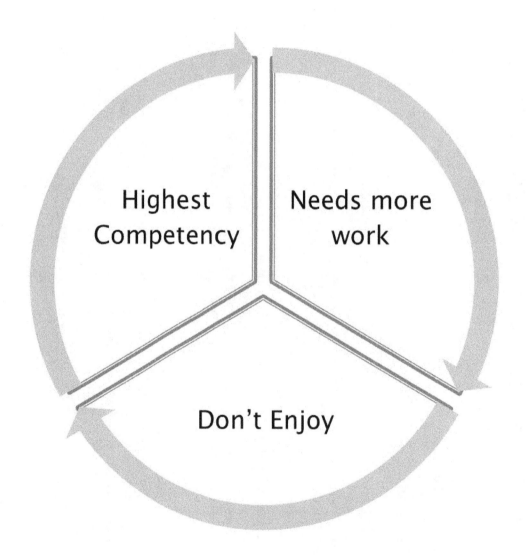

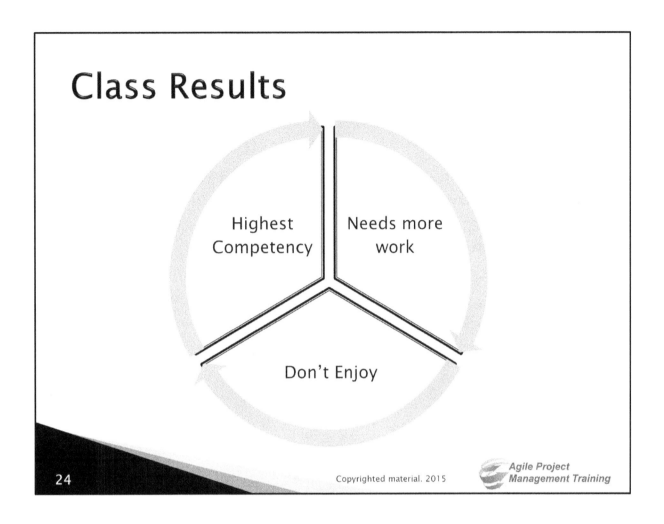

Notes:

Agile Knowledge...

▸ Refer often to the Agile Manifesto
▸ Read the latest books, blogs, podcasts and webinars by industry leaders; Mike Cohn, Ken Schwaber, Jeff Sutherland, Martin Fowler, Alistair Cockburn, Esther Derby, Lyssa Adkins...
▸ Attend Agile conferences and Meetups
▸ Join societies: Agile Alliance, Scrum Alliance, Lean Systems Society
▸ Pursue certifications: CSM, PSM I, PSM II, PMI–ACP, CSP

25

Copyrighted material. 2015

Agile Project Management Training

Notes:

Technical Skillset...

- ▸ Software Developer: Craftsmanship, Code Katas, Open Source Contribution
- ▸ Business Analyst: IIBA, BPMN
- ▸ Test / QA: ISTQB, Exploratory testing, Automation skills, Specification By Example, Testing communities,
- ▸ Project Manager: PMI, Servant leadership, Team dynamics
- ▸ System Engineer: Technical Certifications, ITIL, DevOps

...or whatever skills will make you better at your key role

26

Copyrighted material. 2015

Agile Project
Management Training

Notes:

Business Experience...

- Develop Business Domain knowledge: Market awareness, future trends and directions
- Financial management skills
- Marketing skills
- Human Resources skills
- Learn Agile Business Processes: Agile in the Business, Lean Startup, Agile Business Process Management

27

Copyrighted material. 2015

 Agile Project Management Training

Notes:

Facilitation Skills...

- Techniques: Brainstorming, Icebreakers, Affinity Mapping, Wisdom of the Crowd, Futurespectives
- Achieving session goals and objectives
- Being neutral / impartial
- Keeping focus
- Achieving consensus with conflicting priorities and opinions
- Keeping decisions and actions visible

28

Copyrighted material. 2015

 Agile Project Management Training

Notes:

Affinity Mapping

‣ Use affinity mapping in a workshop environment when you want participants to work together identifying, grouping and discussing issues.

‣ The affinity diagram organizes ideas with following steps:

  ◦ Record each idea on cards or notes.

  ◦ Look for ideas that seem to be related.

  ◦ Sort cards into groups until all cards have been used.

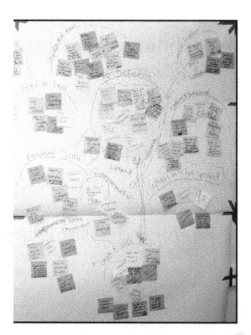

29

Copyrighted material. 2015

*Agile Project
Management Training*

Notes:

| |
| |
| |
| |
| |
| |
| |
| |

Futurespectives

▸ In a futurespective you imagine that you are in the future, at the end of the project, and that you are performing a project retrospective to find out what contributed to the successful delivery of the project.

▸ Goal of a futurespective :
  ◦ What *will we do more of* in the future?
  ◦ What *will we do less of* in the future?
  ◦ What are the things we're not sure about and will monitor going forward?

30

Copyrighted material. 2015

Agile Project Management Training

Notes:

Wisdom of the Crowd

‣ The wisdom of the crowd is the process of taking into account the collective opinion of a group of individuals rather than a single expert to answer a question.
  ◦ Planning Poker
  ◦ Retrospectives

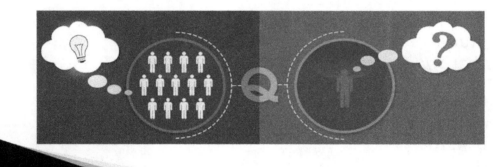

31

Copyrighted material. 2015

Agile Project
Management Training

Notes:

Training Skills...

- ▸ Matching learning to content and audience
- ▸ Teaching through demonstration: "Training from the Back of the Room"
- ▸ Games: Innovation Games, Gamestorming, Tasty Cupcakes
- ▸ Mentoring post-training
- ▸ Alternative delivery methods

32

Copyrighted material. 2015

Notes:

| |
| |
| |
| |
| |
| |
| |
| |

Coaching Skills...

Coaching Models:
- ‣ GROW Coaching Model
- ‣ RESULTS Coaching Model
- ‣ CLEAR Model

33

Copyrighted material. 2015

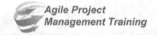
Agile Project
Management Training

Notes:

Notes:

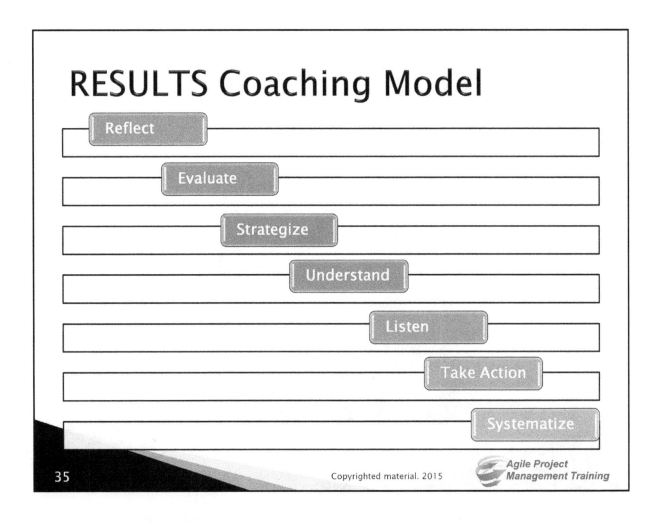

RESULTS Coaching Model

Reflect

Evaluate

Strategize

Understand

Listen

Take Action

Systematize

35

Copyrighted material. 2015

Agile Project Management Training

Notes:

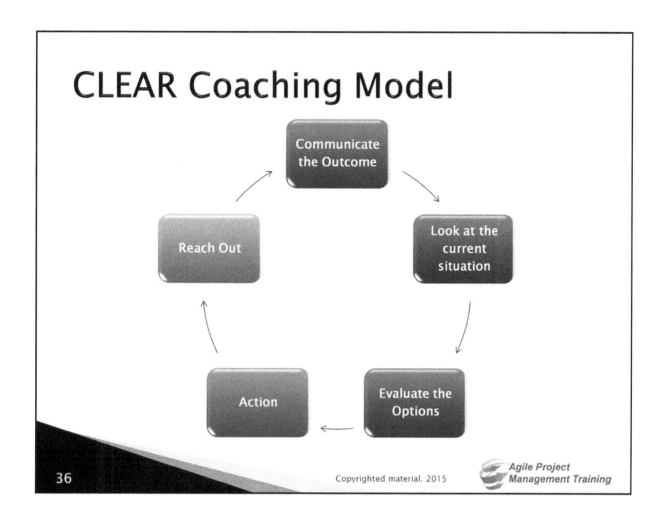

Powerful Coaching Questions

- They are truly open ended
- They are not asked with a "correct" answer in mind
- They invite introspection
- They may present additional solutions
- They almost always lead to greater creativity and insight

37

Copyrighted material. 2015

 Agile Project Management Training

Notes:

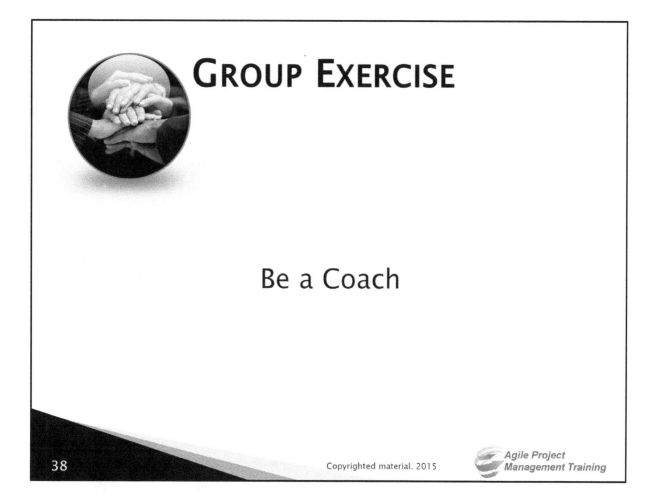

GROUP EXERCISE

Be a Coach

38

Copyrighted material. 2015

Agile Project
Management Training

Notes:

Activity: Be a Coach

Directions:
1. Divide into groups of three
2. Review the scenarios. Each participant picks one and takes a turn playing the coach, team member, and observer.
3. The coach interacts with the team member for 3-5 minutes. The coach can choose to follow the GROW model on the next page or use an approach they are comfortable with.
4. The team member acts out the scenario
5. The observer documents their feedback based upon the following questions:
   1. Which of the competencies of an effective coach were demonstrated in this exercise?
   2. What did the team member do well in interacting with the coach?
   3. Were there opportunities for improvement?

Scenarios:

1. A team member comes to you complaining that a new member on the team is a "slacker." She says, "Joan makes herself scarce and almost never offers to help her teammates, even when we see her doing nothing. I've had it!"

2. The team has been busy all day. All Sprint they have been experiencing a consistently moderate to high workload. You observe a team member of the who appears to be overwhelmed by the task requirements. None of the teammates have come to offer him assistance, so you assume that they are equally busy with their own patients. He appears to "suck it up" and do the best he can.

3. You observe a confrontation where a architect has just reprimanded a developer for moving her code to production without notifying him. The developer is upset and embarrassed but later states that she has experienced this side of the architect before. She decides it is not worth discussing with him because he never listens anyway.

4. During the Sprint Planning meeting, Jim. one of the developers, loses patience with the product owner, "I am tired of these vague User Stories. I have no idea what you want, and I don't get feedback until I am done. This Scrum thing is a waste of time." The Product Owner just looks at you and throws up their hands.

GROW Coaching Model

1. **Establish the Goal**
   - First, you and your team member need to look at the behavior that you want to change, and then structure this change as a goal that she wants to achieve.
   - How will you know that your team member has achieved this goal? How will you know that the problem or issue is solved?
   - Does this goal fit with her overall career objectives? And does it fit with the team's objectives?

2. **Examine the Current Reality**
   - Next, ask your team member to describe his current reality.
   - As your team member tells you about his current reality, the solution may start to emerge.
   - Useful coaching questions in this step include the following:
     - What is happening now (what, who, when, and how often)? What is the effect or result of this?
     - Have you already taken any steps towards your goal?
     - Does this goal conflict with any other goals or objectives?

3. **Explore the Options**
   - Once you and your team member have explored the current reality, it's time to determine what is possible – meaning all of the possible options for reaching her objective.
   - Typical questions that you can use to explore options are as follows:
     - What else could you do?
     - What if this or that constraint were removed? Would that change things?
     - What do you need to stop doing in order to achieve this goal?
     - What obstacles stand in your way?

4. **Establish the Will**
   - By examining the current reality and exploring the options, your team member will now have a good idea of how he can achieve his goal.
   - The final step is to get your team member to commit to specific actions in order to move forward towards his goal. In doing this, you will help him establish his will and boost his motivation.
   - Useful questions to ask here include:
     - So, what will you do now, and when? What else will you do?
     - What could stop you moving forward? How will you overcome this?
     - When do you need to check-in and review progress? Daily, weekly, monthly?

Finally, decide on a date when you'll both review his progress. This will provide some accountability, and allow him to change his approach if the original plan isn't working.

Coaching Do's and Don'ts

Do...
- Actively monitor and assess team performance
- Acknowledge desired teamwork behaviors and skills through feedback
- Embrace conflict as a sign of growth and development
- Coach by example

Do not...
- Coach from a distance
- Coach only to problem solve
- Lecture instead of coach
- Try to change too much
- Lose objectivity
- Be too theoretical
- Be inflexible
- Avoid tough conversations

39

Copyrighted material. 2015

Agile Project
Management Training

Notes:

ACTIVITY

Coaching Self-Assessment

40

Copyrighted material. 2015

Agile Project
Management Training

Notes:

Coaching Self -Assessment

Competency	One Of My Strengths	Doing Okay On This	Need To Develop This	Lacking This Skill
Communicating Instructions. Showing the person you are coaching how to accomplish the task and clarifying when, where, how much, and to what standard it should be done				
Setting Performance Goals. Collaborating with others to establish short- and long-term goals for performance on particular tasks.				
Providing Feedback Carefully observing performance on individual tasks and sharing these observations in a nonthreatening manner.				
Rewarding Improvement. Using a variety of means to provide positive reinforcement to others for making progress on the accomplishment of important tasks.				
Dealing with Failure. Working with others to encourage them when they do not meet expectations.				
Working with Personal Issues. Listening empathically and without judgment, and offering emotional support for non-work difficulties.				
Confronting Difficult Situations. Raising uncomfortable topics that are impacting task accomplishment.				
Responding to Requests. Consulting with others on an as-needed basis. Responding to requests in a timely manner.				
Following Through. Keeping commitments. Monitoring outcomes of the coaching process and providing additional assistance when necessary.				
Listening for Understanding. Demonstrating attention to and conveying understanding of others.				
Motivating Others. Encouraging others to achieve desired results. Creating enthusiasm and commitment in others.				
Assessing Strengths and Weaknesses. Identifying root causes of individual performance. Probing beneath the surface of problems. Keenly observing people and events. Defining and articulating issues effectively.				
Building Rapport and Trust. Showing respect for others. Acting with integrity and honesty. Easily building bonds with others. Making others feel their concerns and contributions are important.				

Plan for Self-Improvement

1. Which, if any, of these competencies are especially relevant to?

2. Which two or three competency areas do you need to improve most?

3. What's in it for you to better yourself in these areas?

4. What have you tried before?

5. What steps can you take personally to improve in these areas?

6. What support do you need to improve in these competencies?

7. How will you monitor your progress in self-improvement as a coach?

8. Who needs to know about this?

9. How will you tell him or her?

10. What are your first few steps?

Plan for Self-Improvement

Which one are you?

- A Manager?
  - Do you tell them what to do?
- A Trainer?
  - Do you give specific education and advice?
- A Consultant?
  - Do you offer to do it for them?
- A Mentor?
  - Do you show them how to do it?
- A Coach?
  - Do you help them do it for themselves?

.. Or are you a little of everything

41

Copyrighted material. 2015

 Agile Project Management Training

Notes:

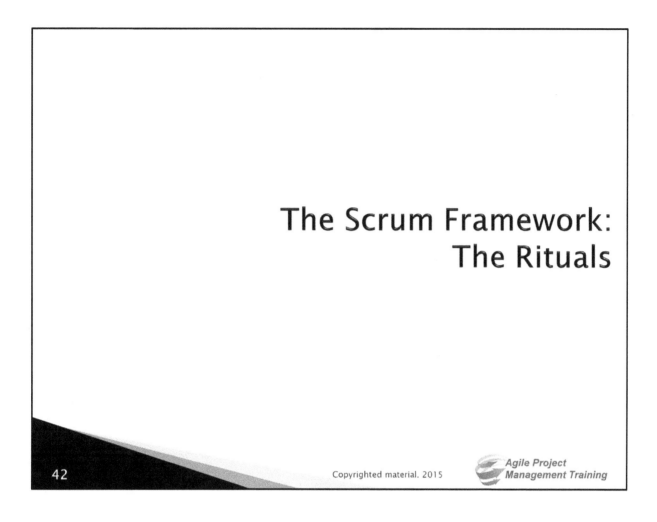

Why all the "rituals"?

▸ These "rituals" are essential to the success of Scrum

▸ There is a reason that the Scrum team should set aside 10% of their total Sprint time on these meetings. They are not simple "overhead administrative" events. They are part of the work and work needs to get done in those meetings.

▸ The reason these meetings are rigidly scheduled and enforced is to provide the structure and rhythm for work to be done.

▸ Structure allows teams to self organize around the "real work" and they trust the rituals and Scrum Master to make sure that everyone is moving along in the same direction.

▸ The meetings allow the project and the team to regulate and redirect itself.

43

Copyrighted material. 2015

Agile Project Management Training

Notes:	

The Rituals

Events	Timebox
Sprint Planning	1 hour/week of Sprint on requirements 1 hour/week of Sprint on design
Sprints	1–4 weeks
Daily Scrum	15 minutes Daily
Backlog Refinement (grooming)	2 hours per week
Sprint Review	1 hour/week of Sprint 1 hour prep
Sprint Retrospectives	3 hours
Scrum of Scrums	2–3 time per week for 30 minutes

44

Copyrighted material. 2015

Agile Project
Management Training

Notes:

Effective Sprint Planning Meetings

- ▸ Backlog grooming is performed in advance of at least two Sprints
    - ◦ By business value
    - ◦ With high-level size estimates
- ▸ Start the meeting with a roadmap review
- ▸ The Product Owner needs to be able to articulate a Sprint Goal
- ▸ The team decides when the User Stories are "good enough" e.g. Definition of Ready

45

Copyrighted material. 2015

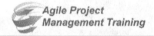
Agile Project Management Training

Notes:

Are your Sprint Planning Meetings Effective?

‣ Does the team own the session, requiring minimal guidance?

‣ Does the team spend some time before the Sprint Planning making sure they are ready to work on the new stories? (i.e. gained knowledge, secured necessary environments, mitigated dependencies, etc.)

‣ Does the team have some ideas for how to get the work done?

‣ Can everyone on the team articulate the Sprint goal?

46

Copyrighted material. 2015

Agile Project Management Training

Notes:

The Sprint

- ‣ Scrum projects progress via a series of Sprints. Sprints are timeboxed to no more than one month.
- ‣ During a Sprint, the Scrum team takes a small set of features from idea to coded and tested functionality.
- ‣ At the end of the Sprint, these features are done; coded, tested and integrated into the evolving product or system.

47

Copyrighted material. 2015

Agile Project Management Training

Notes:

Four-week Sprint

Pros:

- **Very easy to roadmap.** Long-term, one-year roadmaps are much easier when you only have to plan 12 iterations.
- **Low process load.** The key Scrum meetings only once per month, your team is spending less time in meetings and more time building.

Cons:

- **Long turnaround time.** A new idea that comes in the day after a Sprint kickoff can't be started for a month and wouldn't be demoed until a month after that. Two months turnaround time from request to demo can feel interminable.
- **Mini-waterfall.** There is a risk on a four-week Sprint to break up the weeks into design, develop, test, integrate.

48

Copyrighted material. 2015

 *Agile Project Management Training*

Notes:

| |
| |
| |
| |
| |
| |
| |
| |

One-week Sprint

Pros:

- **Fast turnaround time.** At most, a new idea has to wait just a week to start development and a week after that for the first product output.
- **High energy.** One-week Sprints are fun. The energy is high because the deadline is always this Friday. Every week is an end-of-Sprint rush to the finish line.

Cons:

- **Minimal feedback.** There isn't time for a lot of customer feedback before delivering code.
- **Lack of a roadmap.** When your horizon is a week it is difficult planning out a year.
- **Story sizing.** It can be difficult to size all Stories to fit into a week.
- **Relatively heavy...or no process.** A one-week Sprint still needs estimation, tasking, demo, grooming, etc. Relative to the size of the Sprint those fixed time costs will now be high. In practice, the Sprint processes get rushed or omitted.

49

Copyrighted material. 2015

 *Agile Project Management Training*

Notes:

DISCUSSION

What is the right Sprint length for you organization?

50

Copyrighted material. 2015

Agile Project
Management Training

Notes:

| |
| |
| |
| |
| |
| |
| |
| |

Purpose of the Daily Scrum

- ‣ To help start the day well
- ‣ To support improvement
- ‣ To reinforce focus on the right things
- ‣ To reinforce the sense of team
- ‣ To communicate what is going on

51

Copyrighted material. 2015

 Agile Project
Management Training

Notes:

Daily Scrum Do's and Don'ts

Do's
- Same place, same time
- Always stand in a circle and / or have Scrum Master stand outside the circle (avoid eye contact)
- Answer all three questions
- Rotate the Facilitator

Don'ts
- Allow being late to become commonplace (pizza money, sing a song)
- Allow the tools to drive the meeting
- Solve issues in the meeting
- Have team members refer to User Story numbers
- Allow non-team members to speak

52

Copyrighted material. 2015

 Agile Project
Management Training

Notes:

Backlog Grooming Tips

- Try to never schedule backlog grooming during the first or last 20% of the Sprint.
- Treat the backlog grooming meeting just like the first part of the Sprint Planning Meeting
- The Product Owner should present enough work to last 2 Sprints beyond the current Sprint.
- Allow Story Splitting and Sizing to occur
- Make sure everyone understands that estimates are not final until Sprint Planning is performed

53

Copyrighted material. 2015

Agile Project
Management Training

Notes:

When is a User Story Ready?

- A story is **clear** if all Scrum team members have a shared understanding of what it means.
- An item is **testable** if there is an effective way to determine if the functionality works as expected. Acceptance criteria exists ensure that each story can be tested, typically there are three to five acceptance criteria per User Story.
- A story is **feasible** if it can be completed in one Sprint, according to the definition of done.
- **Ready** stories are the output of the product backlog grooming work.

54

Copyrighted material. 2015

Agile Project
Management Training

Notes:

| |
| |
| |
| |
| |
| |
| |
| |

Sprint Review Do's and Don'ts

Do's
- ▸ Show the progress against the Product Roadmap
- ▸ Make sure stakeholders are present
- ▸ Prepare in advance for the Sprint Review meeting
- ▸ Ensure it becomes the Product Owner's meeting

Don'ts
- ▸ The Product Owner acts as customer (they should not be seeing anything for the first time)
- ▸ Allow Sprint Reviews to become boring meetings
- ▸ Not showing working and tested software

55

Copyrighted material. 2015

 Agile Project Management Training

Notes:

Sprint Retrospectives

- ▸ Takes place at the end of each Sprint
- ▸ Examines the way work was performed
- ▸ Inspects how the last Sprint went in terms of people, relationships, process, and tools;
- ▸ Identifies and prioritizes the major items that went well as well as potential improvements
- ▸ Creates a plan for implementing improvements to the way the Team does its work

56

Copyrighted material. 2015

 *Agile Project Management Training*

Notes:

Effective Sprint Retrospectives

▸ Allocate enough time for the meeting.

▸ Structure the meeting carefully to ensure the session flows well, from a clear opening through to the definition of actions at the end

▸ Use engaging (and fun) activities throughout the session

▸ Vary those activities each retrospective to ensure that these regular meetings stay fresh and challenge attendees to look at things from a new perspective

▸ Be tenacious when it comes to creating a small number of concrete, actionable tasks at the end of the meeting. These actions are the real value of the retrospective.

57

Copyrighted material. 2015

Agile Project Management Training

Notes:

A Sprint Retrospective Agenda

1. Set the stage
2. Gather data
3. Generate insights
4. Decide what to do
5. Close the retrospective

Esther Derby and Diana Larsen. 2006. *Agile Retrospectives: Making Good Teams Great.*

58

Copyrighted material. 2015

Agile Project Management Training

Notes:

1. Set the Stage

- ‣ Why we are doing the retrospective
- ‣ Get people talking – do an ice breaker
- ‣ Outline the approach and agenda
- ‣ Establish working agreements

59

Copyrighted material. 2015

 Agile Project Management Training

Notes:

2. Gather Data

- Timeline
  - Create a timeline on flashcard of significant events
- Color Code Dots
  - Team members use sticky dots to show events on the timeline where emotions ran high or low.
- Mad, Sad, Glad
  - Individuals use sticky notes to describe times during the Sprint where they were mad, sad, or glad.
- Fist of Five – Happiness Metric
  - People raise their hand in response to how satisfied they were with the last Sprint. Fist: not at all, 5 fingers: very happy

60   Copyrighted material. 2015    *Agile Project Management Training*

Notes:

3. Generate Insights

- ▸ Brainstorming
  - ◦ Strive for quantity
- ▸ Force Field Analysis
  - ◦ Identify forces for and against change
- ▸ Five Whys
  - ◦ As a pair, ask why 5 times when discussing why a problem happened
- ▸ Sailboat
  - ◦ Put sticky note on different parts of a sailboat. Internal factors that slow it down, anchors. External factors that slow it down, headwind. Internal forces that propel it, outboard motor. External forces support it, tailwind.

61

Copyrighted material. 2015

Agile Project Management Training

Notes:

4. Decide What to Do

- ▸ Retrospective planning game
  - ◦ Brainstorm tasks to implement improvement, then sequence, and team members volunteer to work on them
- ▸ SMART goals
  - ◦ Develop improvement goals that are Specific, Measurable, Attainable, Relevant, and Timely
- ▸ Circle of questions
  - ◦ Time-box a Q&A activity while sitting in a circle

62

Copyrighted material. 2015

Agile Project
Management Training

Notes:

5. Close the Retrospective

- ▸ +/− Delta
  - ○ To retrospect on the retrospective and identify strengths and improvements
- ▸ Appreciations
  - ○ To allow team members to notice and appreciate each other. End the retrospective on a positive note.
- ▸ Helped, Hindered, Hypothesis
  - ○ Help the retrospective leader get feedback to improve skills and processes
- ▸ Return on Time Invested (ROTI)
  - ○ Team members to give feedback on whether they spent their time well

63

Copyrighted material. 2015

 *Agile Project Management Training*

Notes:

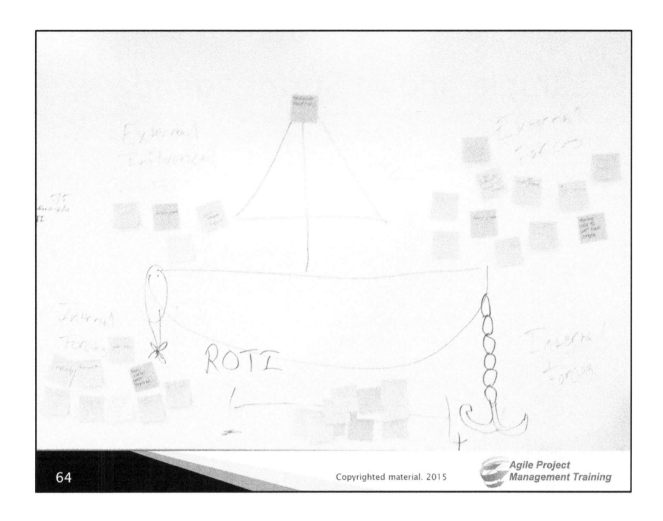

Copyrighted material. 2015

Notes:

Sample end of Sprint agenda

Time	Item (two week Sprint)
9:00–9:15	Daily Scrum (last Scrum of prior Sprint-discuss status of any incomplete stories)
9:15–10:30	Sprint Review Demo of stories delivered over the course of last Sprint
10:30–11:30	Sprint Retrospective focus both on product and process opportunities
11:30–12:30	Lunch
12:30 – 2:30	Sprint Planning Requirements Session: Review Roadmap, Discus Sprint Goal, Review each story in priority order and estimate until velocity is met
2:30–4:30	Sprint Planning Design Session: Team reviews stories, creates tasks for each
4:30–4:45	Team commits to the Sprint Backlog Ready to start Daily Scrum the next day

65

Copyrighted material. 2015

Agile Project Management Training

Notes:

Scrum of Scrums

- Supports multiple teams working on the same product with the intent to address dependent issues
- Each team identifies one person who attends the Scrum of Scrums
- A Scrum of Scrums meets two or three times a week
- The Scrum of Scrums team maintains a backlog of issues and problems to address
- Scrum of Scrums Questions:
  - What has your team done since we last met?
  - What will your team do before we meet again?
  - Is anything slowing your team down or getting in their way?
  - Are you about to put something in another team's way?

66

Copyrighted material. 2015

 Agile Project Management Training

Notes:

Scrum of Scrums Master

- ‣ PatientKeeper delivers to production four times per Sprint
- ‣ Ancestry.com delivers to production 220 times per two week sprint
- ‣ Hubspot delivers live software 100–300 times a day

The Scrum of Scrums Master is held accountable for making this work

67

Copyrighted material. 2015

Agile Project Management Training

Notes:

| |
| |
| |
| |
| |
| |
| |
| |

PAIR UP

Which ritual is easiest?
Which is hardest?
What improvements could you apply in
the next Sprint?

68

Copyrighted material. 2015

Agile Project
Management Training

Notes:

Advanced Requirements Techniques

69

Copyrighted material. 2015

Agile Project
Management Training

Notes:

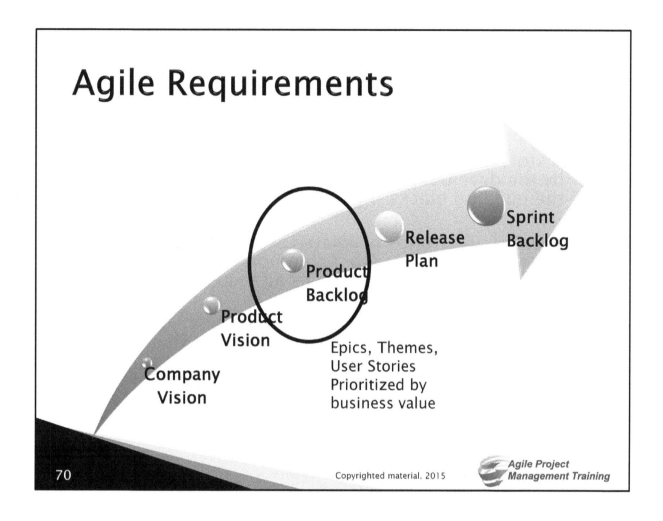

Notes:

Epics, Themes and User Stories

Stories
▸ A story is a self-contained unit of work agreed upon by the developers and the stakeholders. Stories are the building blocks of your sprint.

Themes
▸ Themes are groups of related stories. Often the stories all contribute to a common goal or are related in some obvious way, such as all focusing on a single customer

Epics
▸ Epics resemble themes in the sense that they are made up of multiple stories. As opposed to themes, however, these stories often comprise a complete work flow for a user.

71

Copyrighted material. 2015

Agile Project Management Training

Notes:

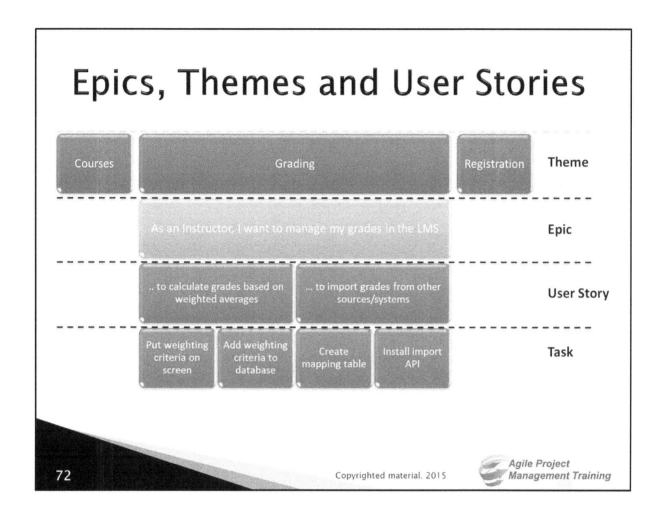

Notes:

Write Epics or User Stories by Role

- ‣ Brainstorm an initial set of user roles
- ‣ Organize the initial set
- ‣ Consolidate roles
- ‣ Refine the roles
- ‣ Prioritize by role

73

Copyrighted material. 2015

 Agile Project Management Training

Notes:

Attributes worth considering when defining roles

▸ Frequency with which user will use software
▸ User's level of expertise with domain
▸ User's general level of proficiency with computers and software
▸ User's level of proficiency with this software
▸ User's general goal for using software

74

Copyrighted material. 2015

Agile Project
Management Training

Notes:

| |
| |
| |
| |
| |
| |
| |

Additional user modeling

▸ Identify personas
  ◦ Fictitious users
  ◦ Should be described sufficiently so everyone on team feels like they know this "person"
  ◦ Choose personas that truly represent user population
▸ Extreme personas
  ◦ Define users who are going to stress the system

75

Copyrighted material. 2015

Agile Project
Management Training

Notes:

Personas

- ‣ Archetypal users of an application
- ‣ Fictitious but based upon knowledge of real users
- ‣ Help guide the functionality and design
- ‣ More accurate User Stories can be written using personas
- ‣ Components of a Persona
  - ◦ Personal profile
  - ◦ Experience
  - ◦ Personal goals
  - ◦ Professional goals

76

Copyrighted material. 2015

 Agile Project Management Training

Notes:

Persona Example

- Jim is 50 years old and works as a mechanic with a company offering road service to customers when their car breaks down. He has worked in the job for the past 10 years and knows it well. Many of the younger mechanics ask Bob for advice. He always knows the answer to tricky mechanical problems.
- He is getting a new computer installed in his van. He doesn't own a computer, and he is a little intimidated by this type of technology.
- He is very nervous that he is going to look stupid if he can't figure it out.

What should you consider when building this system?

Copyrighted material. 2015

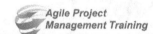
Agile Project
Management Training

77

Notes:					

GROUP EXERCISE

Create an Extreme Persona

78

Copyrighted material. 2015

Agile Project
Management Training

Notes:

Activity: Create an Extreme Persona

Directions:

1. Pick one of the following applications or an internal application and create an Extreme Persona for supporting the requirements process.

   - Exam tool for taking the Scrum Master Certification exam
   - Self-service application for ordering dentures online
   - A simulation software to teach first-time drivers

2. Complete the following table.

3. Be prepared to share your answers with the class

Personal profile	

Technical Requirements

- ▸ Written by development team, architect, tech lead
- ▸ Don't have to be written as User Stories
- ▸ Often part of the Definition of Done
- ▸ Non-Functional Requirements (NFRs) could be part of the Acceptance Criteria

79

Copyrighted material. 2015

Agile Project Management Training

Notes:

Technical Requirements

▸ Examples of technical requirements in the Definition of Done:

  ◦ All code must be peer-reviewed within 4 hours of check-in.

  ◦ If a change is made to the web services interface, the change must be documented on the official web services API wiki page<link to API on wiki>.

  ◦ All code must have automated testing that is consistent with the "Automated Testing Guidelines"<link to guidelines on wiki>

80

Copyrighted material. 2015

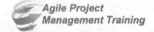
Agile Project
Management Training

Notes:

Technical Requirements

▸ Examples of NFR in acceptance criteria:
  ◦ The system responds to all non search requests within 1 second of receiving the request.
  ◦ The system responds to all search requests within 10 seconds of receiving the request.
  ◦ The system logs a user out after 10 seconds of inactivity and redirects their browser to the home page.
  ◦ Any time a person's credit card number is shown in the application, only the last 4 .digits display

81

Copyrighted material. 2015

Agile Project
Management Training

Notes:

| |
| |
| |
| |
| |
| |
| |
| |

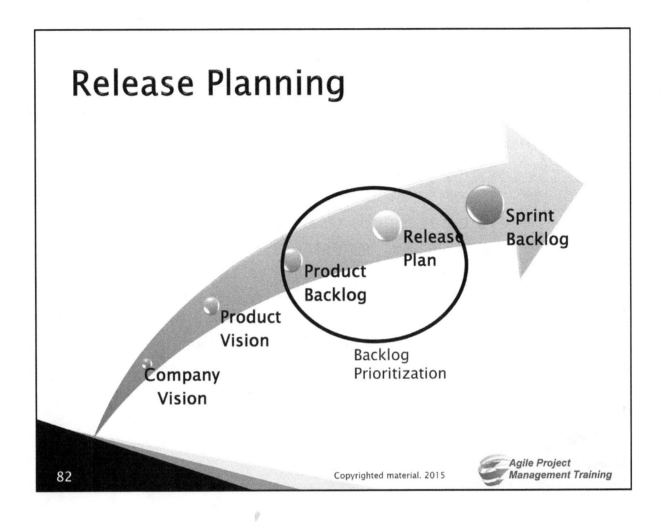

Notes:

Prioritize stories in a backlog

▸ The Product Owner prioritizes stories in a backlog

▸ The backlog is prioritized so that the most valuable items have the highest priorities

▸ Prioritization by Release is called the Product Roadmap

83

Copyrighted material. 2015

Agile Project Management Training

Notes:

Prioritization Techniques

- ‣ Cumulative voting (the money game)
- ‣ MoSCoW prioritization
- ‣ Cumulative voting
- ‣ Kano analysis
- ‣ Risk-based prioritization
- ‣ Relative Ranking
- ‣ Pareto analysis
- ‣ User Story Mapping

84

Copyrighted material. 2015

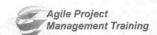

Agile Project Management Training

Notes:

Cumulative Voting

‣ Hundred dollar method
‣ Give each stakeholder $100 in play money and they can "spend" it the requirements they want the most
‣ Can use points, stickers, etc.

85

Copyrighted material. 2015

Agile Project
Management Training

Notes:

MoSCoW Prioritization

Acronym	Description
M – MUST	Describes a requirement that must be satisfied in the final solution for the solution to be considered a success.
S – SHOULD	Represents a high-priority item that should be included in the solution if it is possible. This is often a critical requirement but one which can be satisfied in other ways if strictly necessary.
C – COULD	Describes a requirement which is considered desirable but not necessary. This will be included if time and resources permit.
W – WON'T	Represents a requirement that stakeholders have agreed will not be implemented in a given release, but may be considered for the future.

86

Copyrighted material. 2015

 Agile Project
Management Training

Notes:

Kano Analysis

Need	Definition
Basic	Meets minimum requirements and is a "must have"
Performance	Competitive requirements that the customer "wants", typically an improvement over current system
Excitement	Exceeds customer needs, and a "nice to have"

87

Copyrighted material. 2015

Agile Project Management Training

Notes:

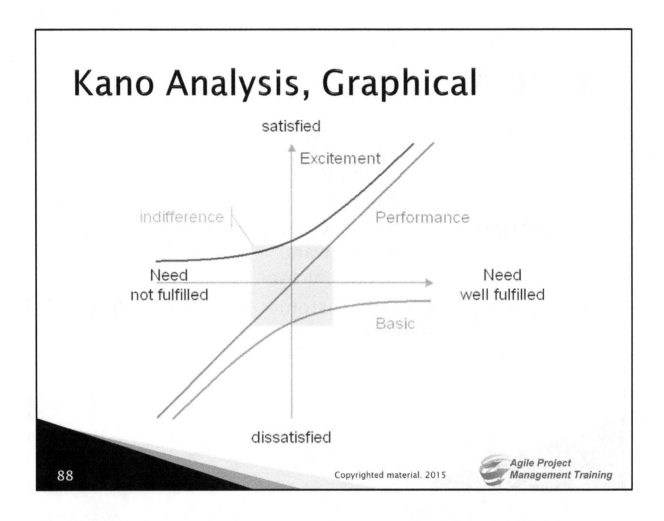

Kano Analysis, Graphical

satisfied

Excitement

indifference

Performance

Need
not fulfilled

Need
well fulfilled

Basic

dissatisfied

88

Copyrighted material. 2015

Agile Project
Management Training

Notes:

Risk-based Prioritization

- Complete high-value, high-risk stories first
- Complete high-value, low-risk stories next
- Complete lower-value, low-risk stories next
- Avoid low-value, high-risk stories

High

2	1
3	X

Value

Low   Risk   High

89

Copyrighted material. 2015

Agile Project
Management Training

Notes:

Relative Prioritization/Ranking

- List all of the requirements
- Estimate the relative benefit
- Estimate the relative penalty
- Determine the total value
- Estimate the relative cost
- Estimate the relative degree
- Calculate priority number
- Sort the list of features by priority

90

Copyrighted material. 2015

Agile Project
Management Training

Notes:

Pareto Analysis

‣ The 80/20 rule

‣ Which 20% of items will yield 80% of the business value?

‣ Used in backlog planning, prioritization, design considerations, etc.

91

Copyrighted material. 2015

Agile Project
Management Training

Notes:

Pareto Analysis

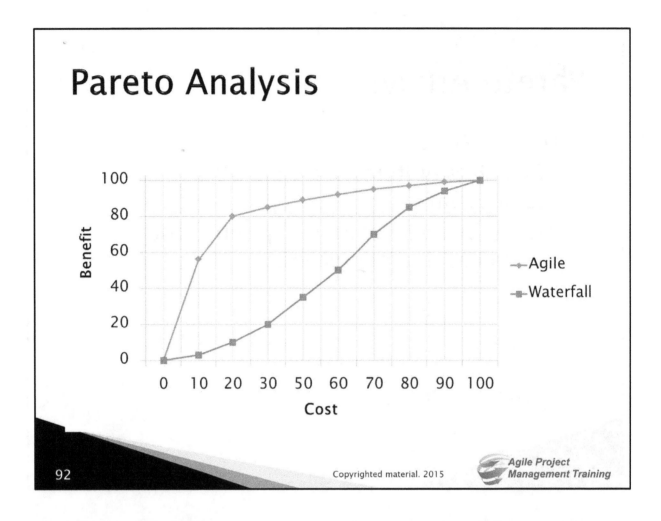

Copyrighted material. 2015

92

Agile Project Management Training

Notes:

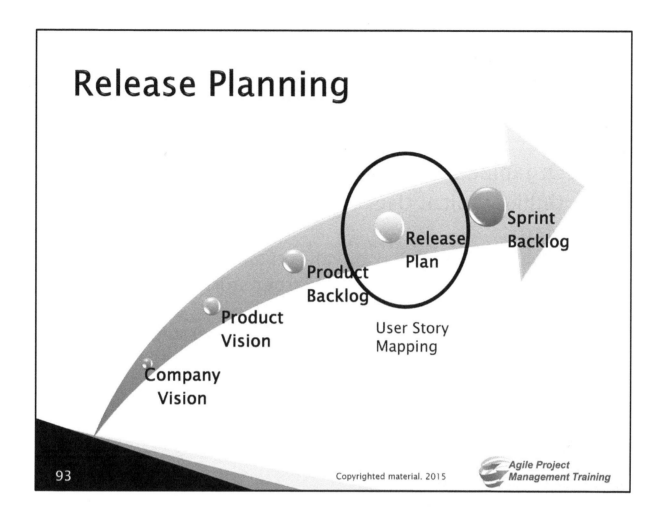

Notes:

User Story Mapping

- User Story Mapping is an approach to Organize and Prioritize User Stories
- Unlike typical User Story backlogs, Story Maps:
  - make the workflow or value chain visible
  - show the relationships of larger stories to their child stories
  - help confirm the completeness of your backlog
  - provide a useful context for prioritization
  - plan releases in complete and valuable slices of functionality.

94

Copyrighted material. 2015

 Agile Project Management Training

Notes:

User Story Mapping: Step 1
Product Roadmap Definition

▸ Spatial arrangement:
- Lay out your product roadmap by major user tasks
- Arrange them left to right in the order you want to make these stories available

95

Copyrighted material. 2015

Agile Project
Management Training

Notes:

User Story Mapping: Step 2
User Story Definition

Arrange the user activities that will be performed within each major task.

| Organize Email | Manage Email | Manage Calendar | Manage Contacts |

| Search Email | File Emails | Compose Email | Read Email | Delete Email | View Calendar | Create Appt | Update Appt | View Appt | Create Contact | Update Contact | Delete Contact |

time ⟶

96

Copyrighted material. 2015

Agile Project Management Training

Notes:

User Story Mapping – Step 3
User Story Decomposition

Overlap user tasks vertically if a user may do one of several tasks at approximately the same time otherwise put them horizontally of the tasks are in sequence.

Below each activity, or large story are the child stories that make it up

Release 1

Copyrighted material. 2015

Agile Project
Management Training

97

Notes:

User Story Mapping – prioritizing

- ▸ Prioritizing based on product goal
  - ◦ Product goals describe what outcome or benefit is received by the organization after the product is put into use
  - ◦ Use product goals to identify incremental releases, where each release delivers some benefit
- ▸ Create horizontal swim-lanes to group features into releases
- ▸ Arrange features vertically by necessity from the user's perspective
- ▸ Split tasks into parts that can be deferred until later releases

98

Copyrighted material. 2015

 Agile Project Management Training

Notes:

| |
| |
| |
| |
| |
| |
| |
| |

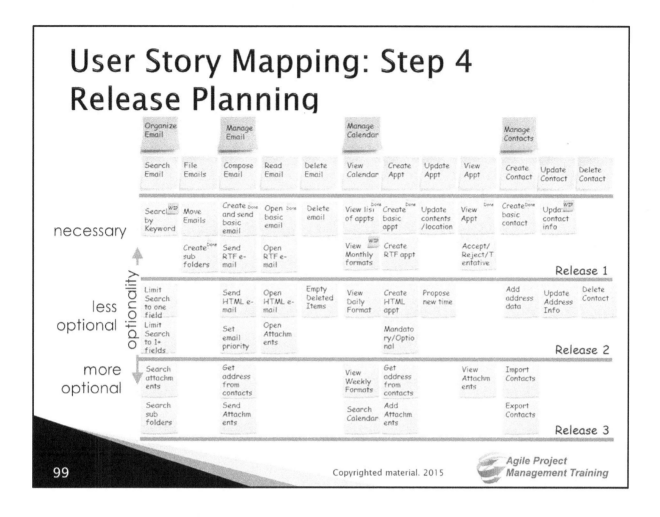

Notes:

Release Options

- Organized around business value
- Internal release versus external release
- Daily builds and continuous integration versus planned release schedule.

100

Copyrighted material. 2015

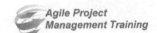

Agile Project
Management Training

Notes:

Sprint Planning

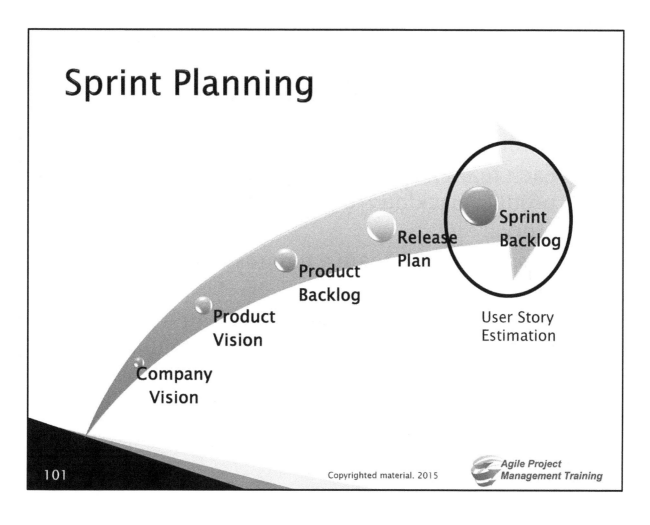

Copyrighted material. 2015

101

Agile Project
Management Training

Notes:

Affinity Estimating

- ‣ Facilitated process
- ‣ Each team member sequences a subset of the product backlog from smallest to largest User Story
- ‣ The rest of the team validates and sequences as a group
- ‣ Bucket the User Stories by a sizing method such as t-shirt size or Fibonacci sequence

102

Copyrighted material. 2015

 Agile Project
Management Training

Notes:

Hours versus Points

- No "right" answer, just be consistent
- A Story point is a universal measurement across the team. It is not biased by the experience or skills or any individual on the team.
- After the 3rd or 4th sprint, the team reaches a rhythm and it becomes easier for the team to quickly estimate the product backlog.
- Mike Cohn* is big on breaking User Stories down into tasks, which are then estimated in hours.
- Mature teams can back into the hours once they have a stable velocity. This is key for budgeting release and contracting with customers.

*Author of Use Stories Applied, 2004

Copyrighted material. 2015

Agile Project Management Training

103

Notes:

Ideal Time versus Elapsed Time

Ideal Time
▸ Used in hour estimating
▸ "Perfect World" estimation approach for a User Story to be completed
▸ Excludes non-programming time
▸ Assumes no interruptions

Elapsed Time
▸ Used in Story Point estimating
▸ Actual time for User Story to be completed
▸ Historical input into better estimates
▸ Key to Velocity calculation

104

Copyrighted material. 2015

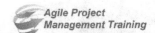
Agile Project
Management Training

Notes:

Burnup Charts

▸ Shows accepted work

▸ Starts at 0 and grows to 100%

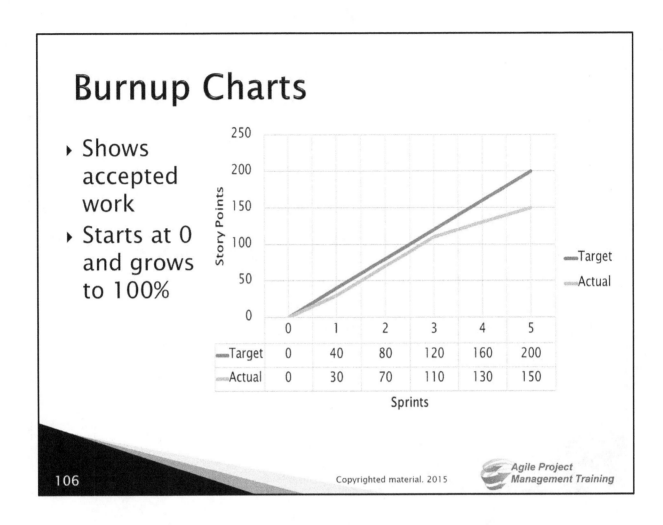

	0	1	2	3	4	5
Target	0	40	80	120	160	200
Actual	0	30	70	110	130	150

Sprints

106

Copyrighted material. 2015

Agile Project Management Training

Notes:

Burndown Bar Charts

▸ Shows net change in work remaining
▸ As tasks are completed, the top of the bar is lowered
▸ When tasks are added to the original set, the bottom of the bar is lowered
▸ When tasks are removed from the original set, the bottom of the bar is raised
▸ When the amount of work involved in a task changes, the top of the bar moves up or down

107

Copyrighted material. 2015

Agile Project
Management Training

Notes:

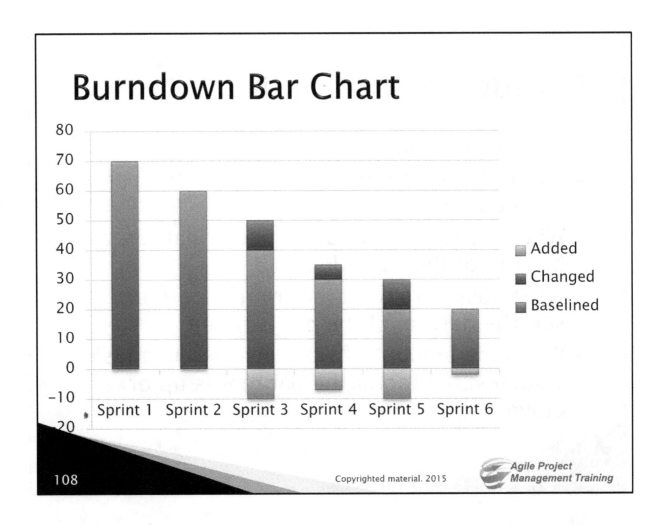

Copyrighted material. 2015

108

Notes:

Cumulative Flow Diagrams

- ‣ Shows work in progress (WIP) in a graphical format
- ‣ Shows the different states of User Stories
- ‣ Can track Kanban states or Scrum states
- ‣ Is an information radiator

109

Copyrighted material. 2015

 Agile Project
Management Training

Notes:

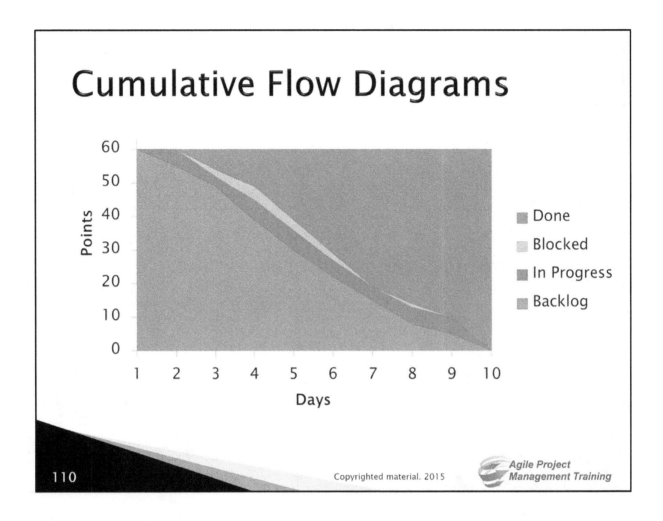

Notes:

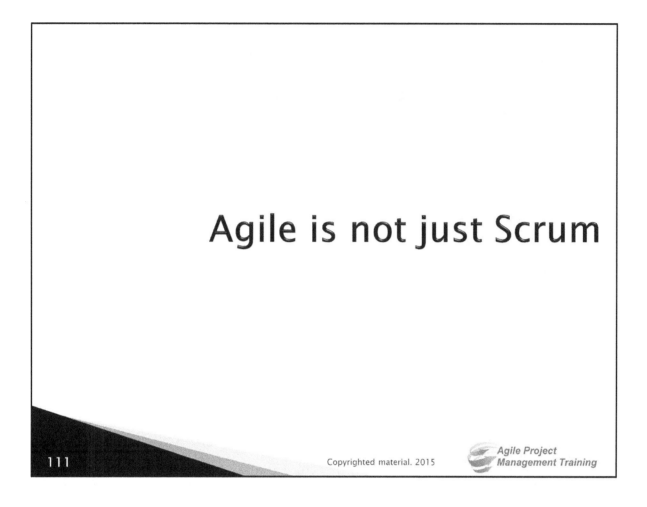

Copyrighted material. 2015

Notes:

Agile Approaches, Principles, Values, Roles and Methods

‣ Scrum
‣ XP
‣ Lean
‣ Kanban
‣ Others...

112

Copyrighted material. 2015

Agile Project
Management Training

Notes:

Scrum Project Management

▸ Scrum is only one of many Agile processes

▸ Agile as an umbrella term that encompasses other processes, such as Extreme Programming, Adaptive System Development, DSDM, Feature Driven Development, Kanban, Crystal and more.

Agile

Lean   Kanban

   XP   RUP

Crystal   Scrum

Copyrighted material. 2015

Agile Project Management Training

113

Notes:

Extreme Programming (XP)

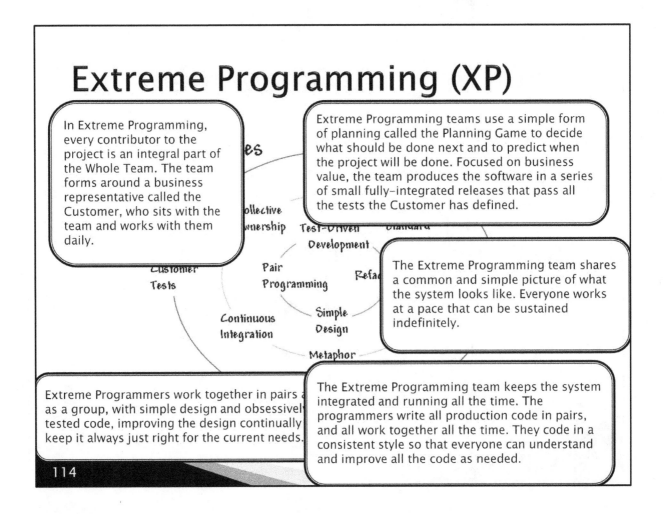

In Extreme Programming, every contributor to the project is an integral part of the Whole Team. The team forms around a business representative called the Customer, who sits with the team and works with them daily.

Extreme Programming teams use a simple form of planning called the Planning Game to decide what should be done next and to predict when the project will be done. Focused on business value, the team produces the software in a series of small fully-integrated releases that pass all the tests the Customer has defined.

The Extreme Programming team shares a common and simple picture of what the system looks like. Everyone works at a pace that can be sustained indefinitely.

Extreme Programmers work together in pairs as a group, with simple design and obsessivel tested code, improving the design continually keep it always just right for the current needs.

The Extreme Programming team keeps the system integrated and running all the time. The programmers write all production code in pairs, and all work together all the time. They code in a consistent style so that everyone can understand and improve all the code as needed.

114

Notes:

| |
| |
| |
| |
| |
| |
| |
| |

Extreme Programming

Whole Team
- In Extreme Programming, every contributor to the project is an integral part of the "Whole Team". The team forms around a business representative called "the Customer", who sits with the team and works with them daily.

Planning Game, Small Releases, Customer Tests
- Extreme Programming teams use a simple form of planning and tracking to decide what should be done next and to predict when the project will be done. Focused on business value, the team produces the software in a series of small fully-integrated releases that pass all the tests the Customer has defined.

Simple Design, Pair Programming, Test-Driven Development, Design Improvement
- Extreme Programmers work together in pairs and as a group, with simple design and obsessively tested code, improving the design continually to keep it always just right for the current needs.

Continuous Integration, Collective Code Ownership, Coding Standard
- The Extreme Programming team keeps the system integrated and running all the time. The programmers write all production code in pairs, and all work together all the time. They code in a consistent style so that everyone can understand and improve all the code as needed.

Metaphor, Sustainable Pace
- The Extreme Programming team shares a common and simple picture of what the system looks like. Everyone works at a pace that can be sustained indefinitely.

115

Copyrighted material. 2015

Agile Project
Management Training

Notes:

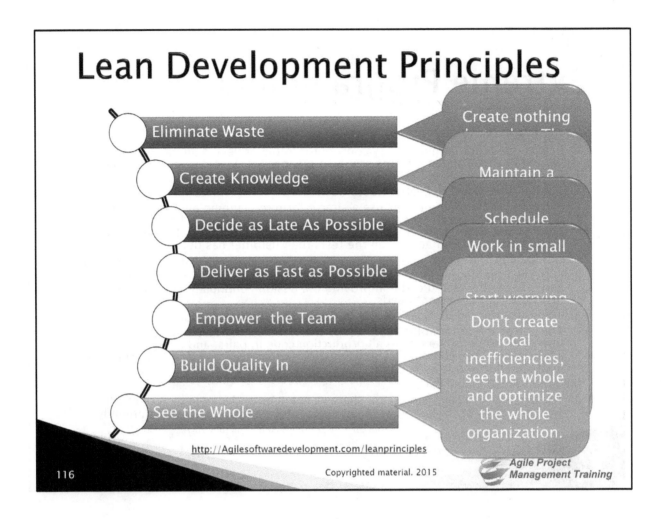

Lean Development Principles

Eliminate Waste
‣ Create nothing but value. The less code you write, the less code you have to test.

Create Knowledge
‣ Maintain a culture of constant learning and improvement.

Decide as Late as Possible
‣ Schedule Irreversible Decisions at the Last Responsible Moment.

Deliver as Fast as Possible
‣ Work in small batches – reduce projects size, shorten release cycles, stabilize work environment.

Empower The Team
‣ Move responsibility and decision making to the lowest possible level.

Build Quality In
‣ Start worrying about it before you write single line of working code.

See the Whole
‣ Don't create local inefficiencies, see the whole and optimize the whole organization.

117

Copyrighted material. 2015

 Agile Project Management Training

Notes:

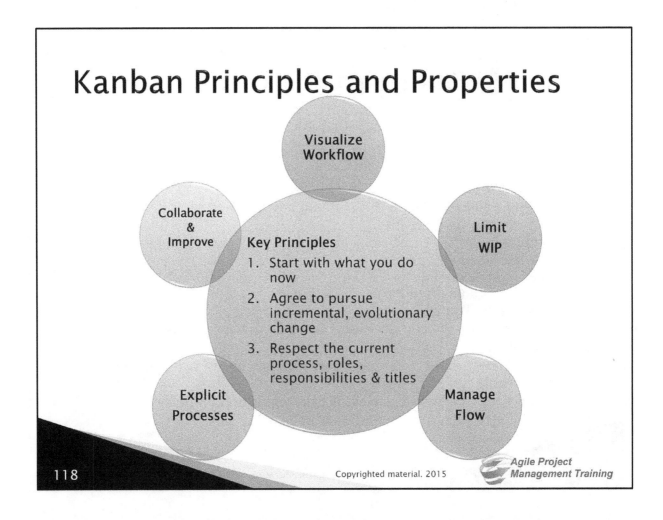

Copyrighted material. 2015

Notes:

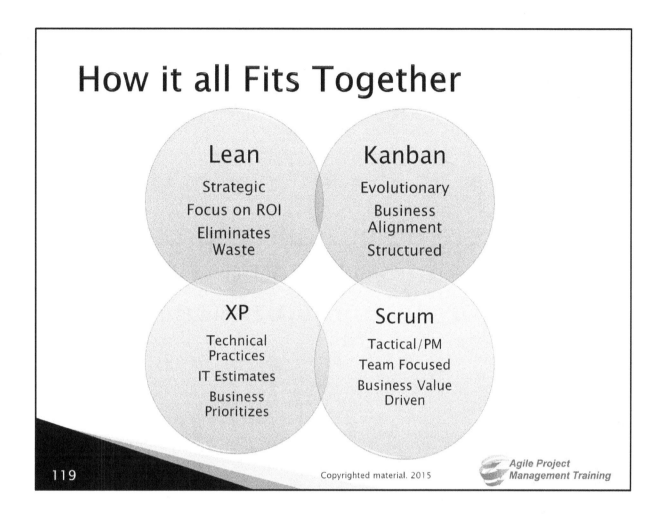

Notes:

DISCUSSION

Are there other Agile approaches than Scrum you should consider for your organization?

120

Copyrighted material. 2015

Agile Project
Management Training

Notes:

Implementing Agile

121   Copyrighted material. 2015   Agile Project
                                                                            Management Training

Notes:

Business Drivers for Scrum

‣ Business climate ripe for change
  ◦ Less willing to invest in long term development
  ◦ Critical mass of successful case studies
  ◦ Everyone is looking for the silver bullet

122

Copyrighted material. 2015

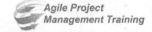 Agile Project
Management Training

Notes:

| |
| |
| |
| |
| |
| |
| |
| |

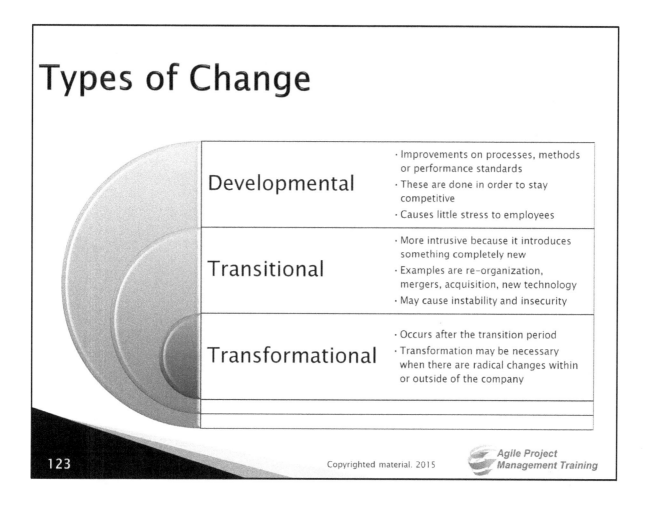

Types of Change

Developmental	· Improvements on processes, methods or performance standards · These are done in order to stay competitive · Causes little stress to employees
Transitional	· More intrusive because it introduces something completely new · Examples are re-organization, mergers, acquisition, new technology · May cause instability and insecurity
Transformational	· Occurs after the transition period · Transformation may be necessary when there are radical changes within or outside of the company

123

Copyrighted material. 2015

Agile Project
Management Training

Notes:

Dealing with Resistance: What to Do

- ☑ Explain the reasons behind the change
- ☑ Identify the advantages
- ☑ Be open for questions
- ☑ Set standards and clear targets
- ☑ Encourage participation and early involvement
- ☑ Recognize and reward efforts
- ☑ Encourage self-management
- ☑ Stimulate creative thinking
- ☑ Seek opportunities the change may bring about

124

Copyrighted material. 2015

Agile Project
Management Training

Notes:

Dealing with Resistance: What <u>Not</u> to Do

- ⊘ Avoid the individual
- ⊘ Lose your confidence
- ⊘ Use aggressive language
- ⊘ Give too many excuses
- ⊘ Threaten
- ⊘ Expect immediate approval or support
- ⊘ Expect to have all the answers at once
- ⊘ Fight with the people resisting
- ⊘ Be obsessive with the details

125

Copyrighted material. 2015

Agile Project
Management Training

Notes:

| |
| |
| |
| |
| |
| |
| |
| |

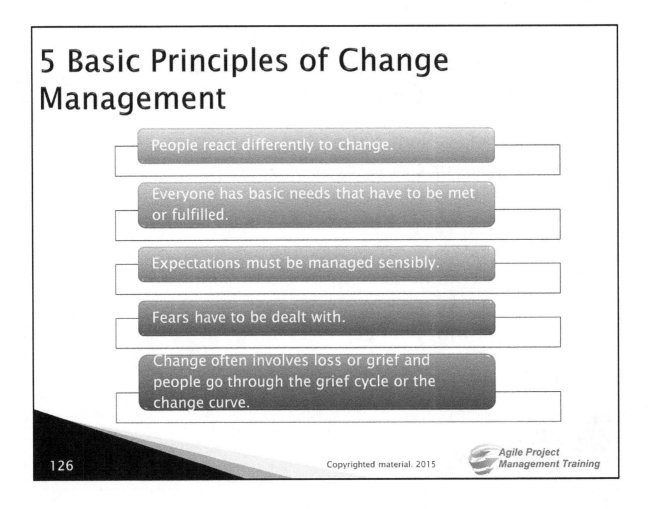

5 Basic Principles of Change Management

People react differently to change.

Everyone has basic needs that have to be met or fulfilled.

Expectations must be managed sensibly.

Fears have to be dealt with.

Change often involves loss or grief and people go through the grief cycle or the change curve.

126

Copyrighted material. 2015

Agile Project Management Training

Notes:

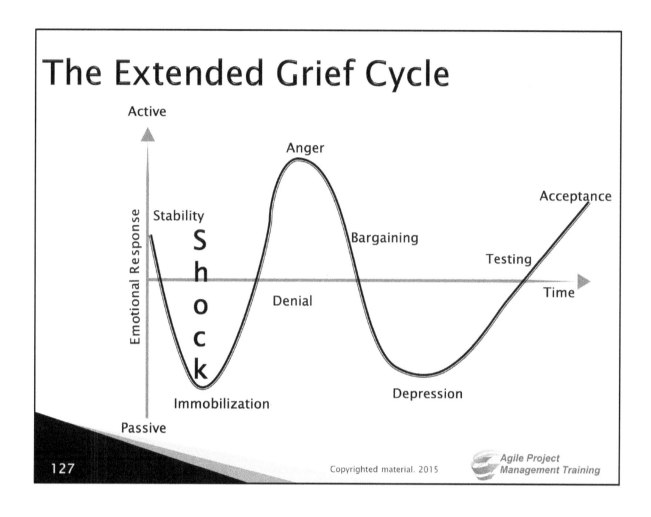

Notes:

DISCUSSION

Where is your organization?

128

Copyrighted material. 2015

Agile Project
Management Training

Notes:

Reasons Why Change Efforts Fail

- ‣ Inability to identify all the urgent reasons for change
- ‣ Failure to point out the one crucial reason for change
- ‣ Lack of commitment
- ‣ Lack of determination
- ‣ Unsuccessful strategizing, execution and comprehension
- ‣ Lack of follow through and control
- ‣ Impatience to see immediate results
- ‣ Inability to adapt and be flexible
- ‣ Resistance overpowers the need to change
- ‣ Fear

129

Copyrighted material. 2015

 *Agile Project Management Training*

Notes:

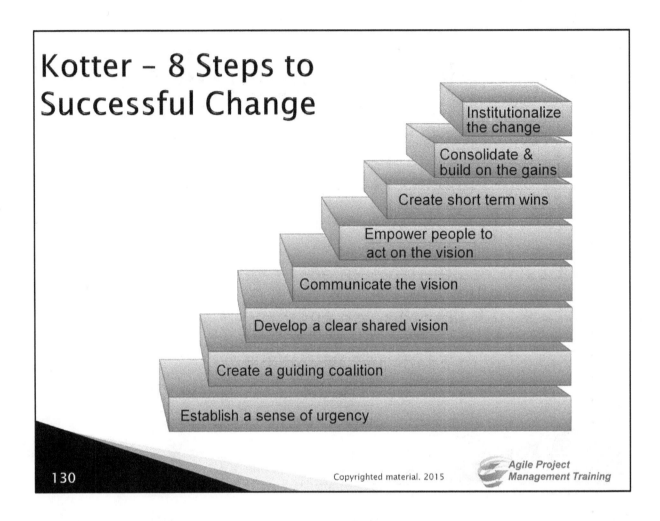

"We are what we repeatedly do. Excellence then, is not an act, but a habit."

Aristotle

Copyrighted material. 2015

Agile Project
Management Training

131

Notes:

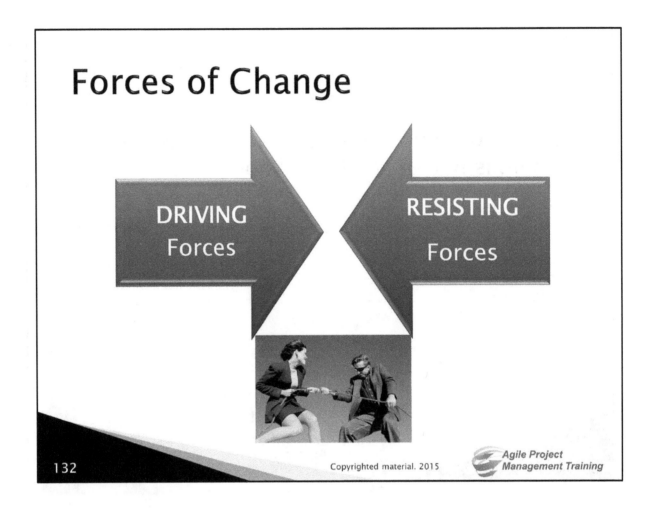

Notes:

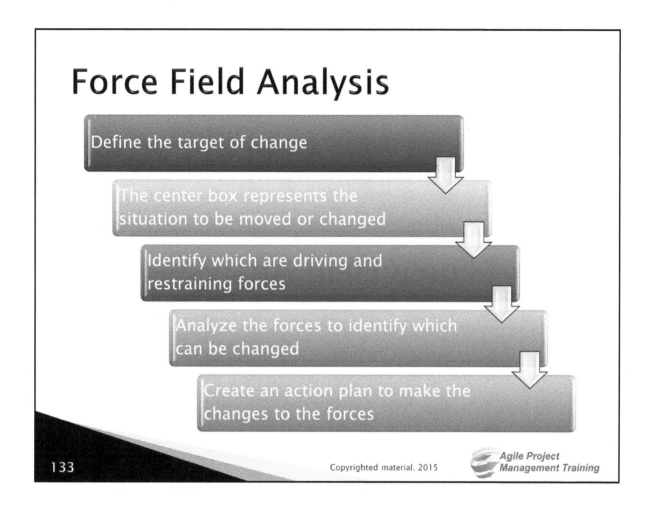

Notes:

ACTIVITY

Force Field Analysis

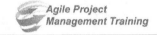

134

Copyrighted material. 2015

Agile Project
Management Training

Notes:

Force Field Analysis

Directions

1. Use the worksheet on the next page.

2. On the center box, the change you are anticipating.

3. List all the forces FOR CHANGE in one column, and all the forces AGAINST CHANGE in another column.

4. Rate the strength of these forces and assign a numerical weight, 1 being the weakest, 5 being the strongest.

5. When you add the "strength points" of the forces, you'll see the viability of the proposed change.

The tool can be used to help ensure the success of the proposed change by identifying the strength of the forces against the change.

ACTIVITY SHEET: *Force Field Analysis*

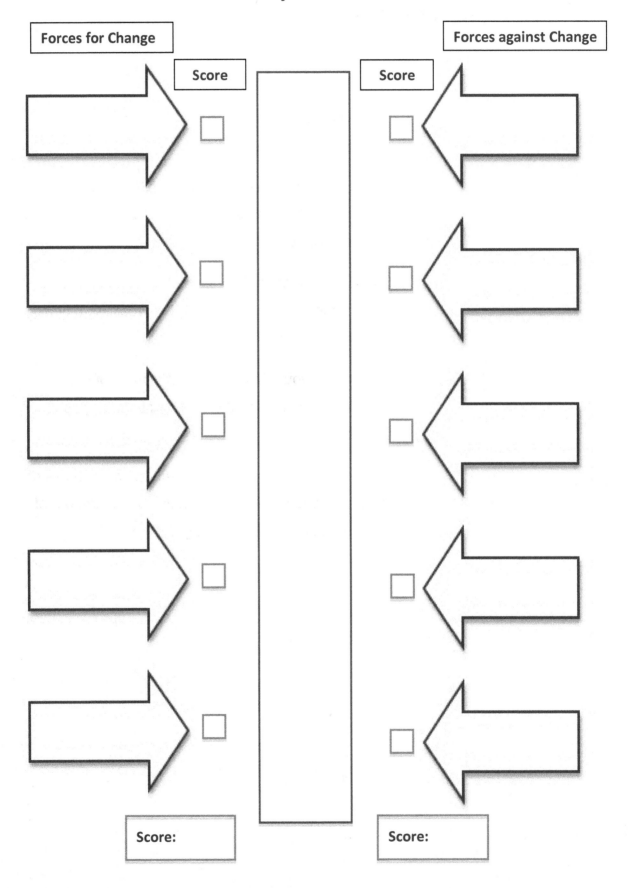

Preparing for PSM I Exam

- ‣ Register for our PSM I Practice Exam for one week or one month.
  - ◦ http://bit.ly/PSMExam
- ‣ You can stop and start as much as you like
- ‣ Take it open book with Scrum Guide
- ‣ Keep taking it until you get 95% correct
- ‣ Actual Exam from Scrum.org requires 85% correct

135

Copyrighted material. 2015

Agile Project
Management Training

Notes:

Differences in Scrum Terminology

PSM I: "Scrum is Immutable"	Alternatives
Scrum Events	Ceremonies, Meetings, Rituals
Backlog Refinement	Backlog Grooming, pre–planning
Daily Scrums	Daily Standups
Scrum Rules	Scrum Best Practices
Sprints	Iterations
Requirements	User Stories
Work Remaining	Burndown Charts, etc.
Mandatory Timebox	Recommendations
No PM	PM as SM
No Gantt's	Iterative Gantts
Cross Functional Team	Specialties such as QA often exist

Copyrighted material. 2015

Agile Project
Management Training

136

Notes:

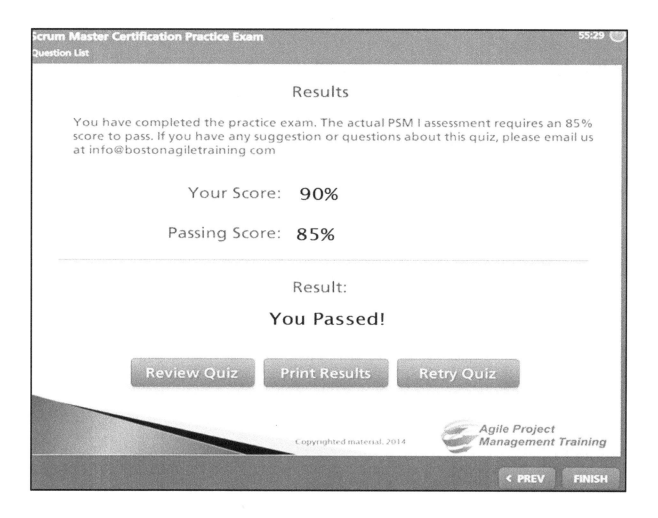

Notes:

ACTIVITY

Agile Review Game
http://bit.ly/ScrumGames

138

Copyrighted material. 2015

Agile Project Management Training

Notes:

Thank-You!

139

Copyrighted material. 2015

Agile Project
Management Training

Notes:

| |
| |
| |
| |
| |
| |
| |
| |

References

- Esther Derby and Diana Larsen. 2006. *Agile Retrospectives: Making Good Teams Great.* Pragmatic Bookshelf
- Ken Schwaber and Jeff Sutherland. 2013. *The Scrum Guide.* http://www.Scrumguides.org and is licensed under a Creative Commons: *http://creativecommons.org/licenses/by-sa/4.0/.*
- Lyssa Adkins. 2010.Coaching Agile Teams: *A Companion for ScrumMasters, Agile Coaches, and Project Managers in Transition.* Addison-Wesley Signature Series
- Mike Cohn. http://www.mountaingoatsoftware.com/blog/why-i-dont-use-story-points-for-sprint-planning
- The Agile Maturity Matrix was adapted from original source: http://www.scribd.com/doc/105468803/Governance-for-Agile-Delivery
- The Scrum Master Competency model was adapted from original source: http://www.slideshare.net/fullscreen/smithcdau/agile-coaching-workshop-13180108/15
- The online Agile self-assessment was adapted from original source developed by Henrik Kniberg and is licensed under a Creative Commons: http://creativecommons.org/licenses/by-nc-nd/3.0/

140

Copyrighted material. 2015

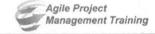
Agile Project Management Training

Notes:

www.ingramcontent.com/pod-product-compliance
Lightning Source LLC
Chambersburg PA
CBHW080421060326
40689CB00019B/4323